Lawrence Wolff

Oleates and oleo-palmitates;

Formic acid as an antiseptic ; Cascara sagrada

Lawrence Wolff

Oleates and oleo-palmitates;
Formic acid as an antiseptic ; Cascara sagrada

ISBN/EAN: 9783337809386

Printed in Europe, USA, Canada, Australia, Japan

Cover: Foto ©ninafisch / pixelio.de

More available books at **www.hansebooks.com**

OLEATES AND OLEO-PALMITATES.

FORMIC ACID AS AN ANTISEPTIC.

CASCARA SAGRADA.

REPRINT OF PAPERS

L. WOLFF, M.D.

PHARMACEUTICAL CHEMIST,

TWELFTH AND CHESTNUT STREETS,

PHILADELPHIA.

PHILADELPHIA:

MERRIHEW & LIPPERT, PRINTERS, 501 CHESTNUT STREET.

1881.

OLEATES AND OLEO-PALMITATES.

By L. Wolff, M.D.

Read at the Phamaceutical Meeting, Phil. Coll. Pharm., October 1881.

Since the publication of my article on Oleic Acid and the Oleates, "American Journal of Pharmacy," 1879, page 8, there has been much written on the subject of the oleates and much complaint made of their instability, their indefinite character and, above all, their price. That the oleates were destined to play a most important part amongst therapeutics, and largely applicable for dermic medication instead of many of the unsightly and often inert ointments in use until now, is a fact that cannot well be disputed. That a substance which is applied to the cutaneous surface, dissolved in the vehicle containing it, will prove more efficacious, by penetrating deeper into the tissues than an insoluble powder distributed on the surface can also not be denied.

When the oleates were first proposed on theoretical grounds, and introduced in medicine, they were thought to be the desiderata by which dermic medication could be accomplished ; but alas, like many *a priori* conclusions, the practical results, while in many instances very satisfactory, left in general much to be desired.

The cause of this is possibly largely attributable to the fact that, so far, our oleates have been of a character scarcely entitling them to that name, for a solution of a metallic oxide in acid without a reaction or the presence of water cannot be considered a salt according to the present views of chemical knowledge. That they are oleic solutions and, as such, of therapeutic value is, however, not to be disputed, though even as such they are of indefinite strength, if we take the so-called oleate of mercury as example, for when the proper amount of mercuric oxide is added only a small quantity of it remains in solution while the greater part, especially if the acid is not pure, is very soon reduced to metallic mercury and, as such, precipitated. If such is the case with pure oleic acid, it certainly is much more so with the oleic acids found in the market, of which the greater portion is the oleo-stearic acid of the candlemakers, deprived of its coloring matter, while others are oleo-palmitic acids derived from either precipitating olive-oil or almond-oil soaps. Either of them soon gives rise to heavy precipitates, as the oleic acid itself has a tendency to take up the oxygen of the oxide and reduce it to the metallic state. Oleic acid, if pure and freshly made, will keep considerable of the oxides in solution, but the very excess of oleic acid present is the cause of its gradual change and deterioration, and though the appearances of the preparation may be saved by repeated filtration, the result is very soon that of an oleate containing no metallic salt in solution.

Actuated by the desire to prepare true oleates, and to obtain them by a cheaper method than the retrograde process of first making acid from a true oleate and then making a series of oleic solutions, led me to experiments of which I already spoke in one of our last year's meetings.

I have already mentioned the fact in my former paper on this subject, that petroleum benzin was a ready solvent for oleates, while it appeared to be a non-solvent, or at least a very limited one at ordinary temperature, of palmitates and stearates. I had utilized this to separate the lead oleate from the lead palmitate in making oleic acid. That chemically true oleates could be made in the same way as the lead oleate in that process was an inference which could be readily drawn, but which proved practically of not much success. As soaps, however, could be readily decomposed by metallic salts into sodium or potassium salts and oleo-stearates or oleo-palmitates of the metals there was no difficulty in obtaining the joint salts which could be separated in turn by the use of benzin. After conducting experiments on that subject, I found that this method of preparing oleo-stearates had been proposed in an article—translated from a French journal—in the "Medical Times," and reprinted in the "American Journal of Pharmacy," January, 1874, page 28.

In order to obtain true oleates, I saponified pure oleic acid, prepared according to my method, as published in my former article, with caustic soda until saponification was complete, dissolved the sodium oleates so obtained in water and precipitated with metallic salts with the results of obtaining oleates that were stable and definite in character, possessing besides therapeutic properties of which I satisfied myself by the experiments which some of my medical friends conducted in hospitals and dispensaries. As oleates prepared in this manner, however, possessed the disadvantage of a high price, I used consecutively soap of the oil of sweet almonds, and ultimately the ordinary castile soap, with quite as much success.

My process in general for obtaining oleates is as follows: One part of castile soap (sodium oleo-palmitate) is dissolved in eight parts of water, the solution so obtained is allowed to cool and stand for 24 hours, when there will be a considerable deposit of sodium palmitate, while the supernatant liquor, containing mostly sodium oleate, is drawn off and then decomposed with a concentrated solution of a metallic salt which, if obtainable, should contain no free acid to prevent the formation of free oleo-palmitic acid. The heavy deposit of oleo-palmitate so derived is strained off, pressed out in the strainer and the adherent water evaporated in a water-bath; after this it is dissolved in about six to eight times its quantity of petroleum benzin and the insoluble palmitate is left to subside while the solution of oleate decanted therefrom is filtered off. The benzin evaporated will yield an oleate that is entitled to that name, as it is a chemical combination and will remain stable and efficacious.

The oleates, so prepared, present an amorphous appearance, while the palmitates are of a crystalline character. While I have noticed a marked affinity of some of the metallic salts for palmitic acid, the absence of it in others is remarkable. Thus, mercury, zinc, bismuth and lead combine with palmitic acid abundantly, but iron and copper seem to form an exception herefrom, and while the oleates of mercury, iron and copper seem to be desirable as therapeutic agents, the oleo-palmitates of zinc, bismuth and lead appear preferable. To take up each one of the above-named alone, I would state that the oleo-palmitate of zinc is a pulverulent substance, imparting a greasy touch, not unlike that of powdered soapstone, and will readily dissolve in warm oils, cosmolin, etc., imparting to them a semi-diaphanous appearance on cooling. One part dissolved in five of cosmolin makes an ointment of zinc oleate, of which I have heard much praise in eczema and other dermic affections. Applied dry to excoriated and erythematous surfaces it acts mechanically by relieving friction, and by its astringent properties it helps to correct and heal the parts. It is prepared by precipitating the soap solution with zinc sulphate.

The oleo-palmitate of bismuth is of an unctuous consistence, and I am advised has yielded very good results in chronic skin affections where an alterative action seems desirable. To prepare it the solution of soap was decomposed by a glycerin solution of the crystallized nitrate of bismuth.

The oleo-palmitate of lead is nothing more than the lead plaster of old, but it is free from glycerin, beautifully white, and dissolved in olive oil makes a litharge ointment more elegant and quicker than the recently-proposed process of precipitating the hydrated oxide of lead from the basic lead acetate solution, and saponifying it with olive oil in the presence of water. It affords also a very excellent substitute for the old lead plaster, and can readily be made in a very short time at an expense not exceeding that of the old method. It is best prepared by precipitating the soap solution with the officinal solution of lead subacetate.

The oleate of mercury is well-known for its therapeutic application, and I dwell on it no further than to state that it should be diluted with cosmolin, unless it is needed to make a marked mercurial impression. It should be prepared by precipitating the soap solution by a concentrated watery solution of mercuric chloride. The precipitate so formed should be heated to the boiling point to insure its subsidence. It is then deprived of its water in a water-bath, dissolved in benzin and filtered, and the filtrate left to evaporate.

The oleate of copper is as yet not used, but I should think would, if diluted with oil or cosmolin, make an excellent stimulant application to indolent ulcers, lupus, etc. The soap solution, precipitated with a solution of cupric sulphate, yields it readily.

The oleate of iron has as yet found no use, to my knowledge, though in the formulas proposed for ferrated codliver oil this is evidently formed. That a definite quantity of it dissolved in codliver oil would serve quite as well, seems obvious, though its odor and taste is not encouraging. I have made it by precipitating the soap solution with a solution of ferrous sulphate, but found that from a ferrous the new-formed salt readily changed to the ferric state.

I have still a number of other metallic salts under experimentation, the results of which I intend to make the subject of another paper. While I do not consider that I have by far exhausted the research in the direction of these valuable therapeutic agents, I trust that I have re-awakened the interest therein which, from incompleteness, began to flag, and that hereafter the oleates will be considered rather as chemically defined bodies than mere unstable solutions of metallic oxides in oleic acids.

Philadelphia, October, 1881.

FORMIC ACID AS AN ANTISEPTIC.

By L. Wolff, M.D.

Read at the Meeting of the Pennsylvania Pharmaceutical Association, June 15, 1881.

QUERY No. 13.—It has been asserted that "formic acid" is a powerful antiseptic. Can these claims be sustained by a series of experiments, testing it by comparison with thymol, carbolic acid and others?

The answer to this query involves the consideration of the processes known as fermentation and putrefaction, which bring about such changes of organic compounds that their atomic relations as well as their chemical character are totally altered or destroyed.

Agents destined to preserve them from these metamorphoses are termed, as a contradistinction of septic change, antiseptics.

If we look at the septic process in organic bodies we always find two factors as conditions for its existence. The first, the passive, is the base, while the second is constituted as an exciting cause or foreign element in the process, and is termed the ferment.

These ferments, although the object of speculation and observation of many able investigators and scientists are as yet not clearly understood as regards their intimate action on, or chemical relation to, fermenting bases. While some are claimed to belong to the lowest type of animal life, others are distinctly vegetable in their existence. While they are again argued to be creations of extraneous influences, chemical, atmospherical, electrical and otherwise, the reasons for conceiving them as part of the result of a process of oxidation are not to be rejected. That they are minute living organisms is certain, as is proved by their structure, development and proliferation.

The presence of water and oxygen of the atmosphere are conditions, however, which are invariably necessary for the septic process, and on the exclusion of these several antiseptic proceedings are based.

Little as the above remarks may seem to bear on the direct solution of our query, they will probably explain, to some extent, the action of the so-called antiseptics hereinafter mentioned.

Antiseptics may be termed all such substances which, by their chemical or organic action, exercise a destructive influence on the lowest type of organic existence. That this is a peculiar and chemically not well explained process or function would result from the fact that such bodies acting destructively on animal and vegetable tissue and existence, are not always found to behave in this manner towards the minute spores and growths of microscopic organisms, while again valuable and powerful antiseptics have but a relatively unimportant effect, if any whatever, on the higher developed animal or vegetable existence.

Formic acid, the subject of consideration in this query, is represented by the symbols $HCHO_2$, and occurs variously in nature, in ants (therefore its name) and some plants, but is best and most easily obtained by decomposing oxalic acid in presence of glycerin and water. It is a colorless liquid of 1·235 sp. gr., and produces violent irritation, and even vesication, if applied to the skin. Diluted with water, it proves less caustic. Internally, it acts as a gastro-intestinal irritant. Its principal therapeutical application is as a local irritant and rubefacient, but it is not employed internally for any corrective or curative purpose. It is not apparent what has caused its repute as an antiseptic in the above sense of the word, for neither its chemical composition and properties, nor its therapeutic action, would speak for this. As, however, the origin of many of our remedies and antiseptics has been obscure and purely empirical, their value as such can only be ascertained by a series of experiments, with a view of demonstrating this point comparatively with other agents of this class. These expe-

8

riments, in order to be reliable, will have to be conducted simultaneously, and under the same influences; for it is a fact to be well borne in mind, that these ferments exciting causes of organic changes are in their development and action subject to the influence of temperature, atmosphere and climate. While in cool and dry climates of mountain regions, as on our western high plateaus, organic decomposition takes place very gradually, and is altogether impossible in the eternal ice of the Arctic, or at the boiling temperature, it goes on with astounding rapidity in the tropics, and their humid atmospheres.

Owing to the difference of the processes of fermentation and putrefaction, and the different exciting causes thereof, antiseptics thus of service in the former would not necessarily be of use in the latter.

The spores composing the fungi of yeast, variously termed torulæ cerevisiæ, saccharomyces cerevisiæ, or mycodemæ, cryptococci, hormiscii, etc., seem the true exciting causes of fermentation, and may require different antiseptics than those of other septic processes.

To test these points, as well as to ascertain the comparative value of formic acid to arrest the action of these fungi, I diluted an aqueous extract of malt, containing glucose, dextrin and diastase, thus composed of all elements necessary for fermentation, largely with water, and exposed it in open vessels at a temperature of between 80° and 90°F., with the following results:

One part extract of malt with four parts of water:

Antiseptic.	Time fermented in.
None,	48 hours
Glycerin, 20 drops,	72 hours
Formic acid, 4 drops,	96 hours
Boracic acid, 2 grains,	108 hours
Benzoic acid, 2 grains,	6 days
Carbolic acid, 4 drops,	10 days
Thymol, 2 grains,	2 weeks
Salicylic acid, 2 grains,	18 days

It will readily be seen from the above that whatever the antifermentive powers of formic acid are they are so feeble as to deserve no consideration as such. I would point to the fact that, recent writings to the contrary, which claim that pure salicylic acid, devoid of phenic acid, possessed no antiseptic properties, it is shown in this table, which presents the average of a series of experiments, that it proved itself superior to any and all, even to carbolic acid, to the presence of which, as a contamination, its antiseptic properties were attributed.

As putrid decomposition of organic bodies is due to different causes, largely of foreign influence, the antiseptics, to prevent this, should probably differ in their action on the factors exciting such decomposition.

It is claimed for this septic process, and well illustrated by microscopic observations, that it is originated and effected through micrococci in the atmosphere invading the substances and thus bringing about in an inexplicable manner their oxidation and decomposition. These bacteriæ, vibriones, zoogloes, monades, mycrocymas, and whatever else they may be called, present the most primitive form of organic life, and it is the destructive effect on them by antiseptics which preserves organic bodies from chemical change and loss of character and form.

To examine an agent as to its utility as an antiputrid can only be accomplished by actual experiment, and for this purpose I have in this case selected as base that highly organized and susceptible substance, approaching protoplasm in its arrangement and character, the white of egg.

One part of white of egg was diluted with one part of water, and to it was added with results as below stated :

Antiseptic.	Time of Decomposition.
4 drops of formic acid,	. 3d day
20 drops of glycerin, .	4th day
None, . .	. 5th day
2 grains boracic acid,	9th day
2 grains benzoic acid,	. 16th day
2 grains salicylic acid,	24th day
4 drops carbolic acid,	. 26th day
2 grains thymol, .	30th day

These experiments were conducted simultaneously, at the same temperature, and are again the average of a number of them. They clearly demonstrate that formic acid has not alone no antiputrid action, but it seems really to invite the averages of bacteriæ and vibriones, thus causing a more rapid decomposition. The same may be said of glycerin, although it has antifermentive powers, which, in the quantities as used in the former experiments, were, however, of but little avail.

As the results of the above and other original experiments, along with research in the literature of this subject, I would respectfully report to the Pennsylvania Pharmaceutical Association that formic acid is not possessed of properties entitling it to the asserted claims as an antiseptic, that it is only a feeble antifermentive and of no value whatever as an antiputrid agent.

CASCARA SAGRADA.

BY L. WOLFF, M.D.

Read at the Meeting of the Pennsylvania Pharmaceutical Association,
June 15, 1881.

QUERY No. 7.—What are the true therapeutic properties of Rhamnus purshiana so-called Cascara sagrada? It is recommended by some as an active cathartic, whilst others assert that it is a very mild laxative, and in order to increase its activity a certain amount of mandrake is added.

Since the above query was accepted there have appeared at various times a number of essays in some of our journals, which tended to clear up many doubts on this subject.

Before entering on the direct answer to the above query I would submit a few remarks condensed from a recent article in "New Remedies":

Rhamnus purshiana, D. C.—Rhamnus aliifolius, Pursh-Frangula purshiana, *Cooper*, the Caseara sagrada, or sacred bark, also Chittem bark of the Mexican settlers of California, is a small shrub of the natural order of Rhamnaceæ, indigenous to the western slope of the Rocky Mountains, ranging between the southern California and the British possessions. The bark is the principal part used in medicine, and has long been known as a mild cathartic to the Mexicans, the native inhabitants of California. It comes in curved pieces or quills, of divers lengths, from one-sixth to one-eighth inch in thickness. Externally, it is nearly smooth, gray, sometimes with whitish patches.

The middle layer is brown to reddish-brown, and the inner is light yellowish to light brown. It presents a smooth fracture, is colored red by potassa, is without odor, and imparts a bitter-sweetish, slightly astringent taste.

The excellent analysis of Dr. A. B. Prescott ("A. J. Ph.") reveals:

1st. A brown resin, sparingly soluble in water, readily soluble in stronger and dilute alcohol, of strong bitter taste, colored purple-red by potassium hydrate; this is mostly contained in the middle and inner layers.

2d. A red resin, nearly tasteless, colored brown by potassium hydrate, insoluble in water, soluble in stronger and dilute alcohol; it is principally found in the outer layer.

3d. A light yellow resin or neutral body, tasteless, not colored by potassium hydrate. It is soluble in hot, sparingly so in cold alcohol of seventy per cent.

4th. A crystallizable body (possibly a product rather than educt), then tannic acid, oxalic acid, malic acid, fat oil, volatile oil, wax and starch.

The resemblance of its composition and structure, as well as its proximate principles to that of the bark of Rhamnus frangula, even if the continued change of one of these bodies into another by glucosic fermentation is conceded, seems to point to the close relation of these species, and shows the reason for their similar action.

As to its therapeutic value, I have found it in a number of cases under observation quite similar to that of Rhamnus frangula, although the latter appears to be the more active of the two, and apt to occasion griping and nausea.

That its laxative or cathartic effect is due to the resins contained therein will appear from the fact that the powder, after being thoroughly exhausted by stronger alcohol, I have found to be utterly inert.

Its physiological action is that of a stimulant to the mucous secretions of the intestines and colon. It imparts to the stomach and bowels, when taken, a sensation of warmth.

By its tonic effect on the muscular fibres of the intestines, and especially on those of the colon, it relieves habitual constipation when due to a lack of peristaltic motion and atony of those fibres. Through its stimulant effect on the mucous surfaces of the intestines it acts also as a mild cholagogue. It increases slightly the secretion of urine, produces in from four to six hours, without exciting the vascular tissue or nerve centres, a number of copious stools, improving the appetite thereby, without manifesting an instant effect on the stomach or intestines, or causing exhaustion. It seems well intended as an evacuant for subjects of sluggish portal circulation, and especially for the sufferers of hemorrhoidal troubles.

While I have not been able to ascertain a probable change in the bark, as is well known to occur in the bark of Rhamnus frangula, for a year or two after being gathered, the inference by its close resemblance to the latter would be in favor thereof, and thus probably the reports of the difference in the action of this drug, as enumerated in this query, may be accounted for.

The dose in which it is employed as a laxative is a half fluidrachm of the alcoholic fluid extract; as a cathartic, from one to two fluidrachms. In comparison to this, I quote that the laxative dose of an alcoholic fluid extract of the one-year-old bark of Rhamnus frangula ought not to exceed twenty drops. A teaspoonful of such a preparation will produce in some persons most violent and hydragogue catharsis.

In answer to that part of the query, if an addition of mandrake would be necessary to increase its activity, I would state that such addition seems for that purpose unnecessary, although it may be useful in hepatic torpor, where a special impression on the biliary secretion seems desirable, and thus its cholagogue action is to be increased.

I would close this answer by stating that, in my experience, and according to the observation of myself and a number of physicians who kindly furnished me with their data for this report, the bark of Rhamnus purshiana, popularly known as Cascara sagrada, is in smaller doses a useful mild laxative of some cholagogue action, and in larger doses decidedly cathartic; that also an admixture of mandrake or other substances to increase its cathartic action seems totally superfluous.

www.ingramcontent.com/pod-product-compliance
Lightning Source LLC
Chambersburg PA
CBHW031159090426
42738CB00008B/1398